WORLD IN
FOCUS

FOCUS ON
CANADA

HEATHER BLADES

WORLD ALMANAC® LIBRARY

Please visit our web site at: www.worldalmanaclibrary.com
For a free color catalog describing World Almanac® Library's list of high-quality books and
multimedia programs, call 1-800-848-2928 (USA) or 1-800-387-3178 (Canada).
World Almanac® Library's fax: (414) 332-3567.

Library of Congress Cataloging-in-Publication Data available upon request from publisher.
Fax (414) 336-0157 for the attention of the Publishing Records Department.

ISBN 0-8368-6215-5 (lib. bdg.)
ISBN 0-8368-6234-1 (softcover)

This North American edition first published in 2006 by
World Almanac® Library
A Member of the WRC Media Family of Companies
330 West Olive Street, Suite 100
Milwaukee, WI 53212 USA

Commissioning editor: Victoria Brooker
Editor: Kelly Davis
Inside design: Chris Halls, www.mindseyedesign.co.uk
Cover design: Hodder Wayland
Series concept and project management by EASI-Educational Resourcing (info@easi-er.co.uk)
Statistical research: Anna Bowden

World Almanac® Library editor: Alan Wachtel
World Almanac® Library cover design: Scott Krall

Population Density Map © 2003 UT-Battelle, LLC. All rights reserved.
Data for population density maps reproduced under licence from UT-Battelle, LLC.
All rights reserved.
Maps and graphs: Martin Darlison, Encompass Graphics

Picture acknowledgements:
The author and publisher would like to thank the following for allowing their pictures to be
reproduced in this publication:
Corbis title page and 24 (Earl and Nazima Kowall), 4 (Staffan Widstrand), 9 (Bettmann), 10, 12
(Sean Sexton Collection), 13, 37, 46, 48, 58 and 59 (Reuters), cover and 15 (Gordon R. Gainer),
16 (Craig Aurness), 17 (Dan Guravich), 20 (Dewitt Jones), 22 and 23 (Jim Young/Reuters), 25
(Carl and Ann Purcell), 26 (Jonathan Blair), 31, 33 and 41 (Paul A. Souders), 32 (l) (Natalie
Forbes), 34 (Jeff Christensen/Reuters), 35 (Joseph Sohm, ChromoSohm Inc.), 36 (Baci), 38 and 57
(t) (Galen Rowell), 39 (Vince Streano), 44 (Wolfgang Kaehler), 45 (Christopher J. Morris), 50
(Gunter Marx Photography), 51 (Laszlo Balogh/Reuters), 56 (W. Perry Conway), 57 (b) Geray
Sweeney); EASI-Images/Roy Maconachie 19 and 40; Mary Evans Picture Library 8 and 11;
Chris Fairclough 5, 14, 21, 27, 28, 29, 32 (r), 42, 43, 47 (l), 47 (r), 52, 53 and 54.

The directional arrow portrayed on the map on page 7 provides only an approximation of north.
The data used to produce the graphics and data panels in this title were the latest available at the
time of production.

Printed in China

1 2 3 4 5 6 7 8 9 10 09 08 07 06

CONTENTS

Cover: A tourist boat approaches the Canadian side of Niagara Falls, which straddles the border between Canada and the United States.

Title page: Demonstrators rally in Montreal against the separation of Quebec from the rest of Canada.

CHAPTER 1

Canada – An Overview

Covering 3,855,081 square miles (9,984,670 square kilometers), Canada is the second-largest country in the world after Russia. From north to south, it extends 2,858 miles (4,600 kilometers), from Alert on Ellesmere Island in the north to the United States border near Detroit, Michigan, in the south. East to west, it stretches 3,418 miles (5,500 km), from St. John's, on the coast of Newfoundland, to the western border with the state of Alaska. Canada is surrounded by three oceans, and each of these oceans influences the country's climate, economy, and trade links. To the north, the cold Arctic remains frozen for much of the year but yields some fur and fish resources; to the west, the Pacific is important for trade links with the growing economies of Southeast Asia; and to the east, the Atlantic gives access to Europe and the United Kingdom (UK). Canada's only land border is with its main trading partner, the United States, and this boundary is the longest undefended land border in the world.

▼ A villager fishes for Arctic char through a hole in the ice, on Baffin Island, in Nunavut.

▲ Pedestrians cross a street in downtown Toronto, Ontario. Like many of Canada's largest cities, Toronto's population is very multicultural.

THRIVING CITIES

The country is made up of seven provinces and three territories that stretch across six different time zones. Its considerable physical size and extreme environments have made settlement difficult, and the country's relatively low population is distributed unevenly. The Northwest Territories and Nunavut, the main wilderness regions, together make up one-third of Canada's total area (about the same size as India) yet contain only sixty thousand people. Most Canadians live in the large cities of Montreal, Toronto, Vancouver, and Ottawa, which are thriving centers of business and leisure. Over 90 percent of Canada's people live in towns and cities close to the United States border. These cities are relatively crowded, with an increasing number of Canadians and immigrants moving to them in search of well-paid employment and a high standard of living.

DIVERSE PEOPLES

Canada has a history of struggles between different groups of settlers, mainly the British and the French, and its indigenous peoples. The country first became a united confederation in 1867, and Canadians mark the event every year on July 1, or Canadian Independence Day. Canada remains predominantly English-speaking, but there is a large percentage of French-speaking Canadians and a mixture of different cultures throughout the country. The indigenous Canadian Indians, more commonly known as the First Nations people, make up only 4 percent of the present population. Around 29 percent of Canadians are of French origin, and the majority of them live in the French-speaking province of Quebec. Most Canadians enjoy one of the highest standards of living in the world, with excellent health-care and education facilities, income, and social welfare programs. However, many First Nations people living on reservations do not share these advantages. Many indigenous people suffer high unemployment and poor health and housing. The suicide rate in First Nations Inuit groups is three times the national average.

As a resource-rich country, Canada is closely tied to the United States as a trading partner. In spite of these close economic ties, Canada has its own dollar currency, which is distinct from the U.S. dollar. Although Canada and the United States have similarities and political ties, Canada maintains closer political ties with Britain—or France in the case of Quebec—than with the United States.

WILDERNESS AREAS

Canada is a country of amazing natural beauty, with wilderness areas making up 60 percent of its land area. Around 10 percent of the world's freshwater is found in a mosaic of lakes, rivers, and ice sheets spread across Canada. In the north, where temperatures rarely climb above 32 °Fahrenheit (0 °Celsius) for much of the year, the subsoil is permanently frozen. Canada's wilderness areas have remained a wildlife haven for many years. They have been only occasionally penetrated by trappers and hunters searching for valuable fur pelts. The golden eagle, with a wingspan of over 8 feet (2.4 meters); the grizzly bear; wolves; and reindeer (or caribou) are just a few of the magnificent creatures found in these remote regions.

Physical Geography Data

- Land area: 3,511,003 sq miles/9,093,507 sq km
- Water area: 344,078 sq miles/891,163 sq km
- Total area: 3,855,081 sq miles/ 9,984,670 sq km
- World rank (by area): 2
- Land boundaries: 5,523 miles/8,893 km
- Border country: United States
- Coastline: 125,492 miles/202,080 km
- Highest point: Mt. Logan (19,551 ft/5,959 m)
- Lowest point: Atlantic Ocean (0 ft/0 m)

Source: CIA World Factbook

 Did You Know?

Quebec is Canada's largest province, with an area of 594,856 sq miles (1,540,680 sq km). It has a population of almost 8 million, and over 5 million of Canada's 6.5 million French Canadians live there.

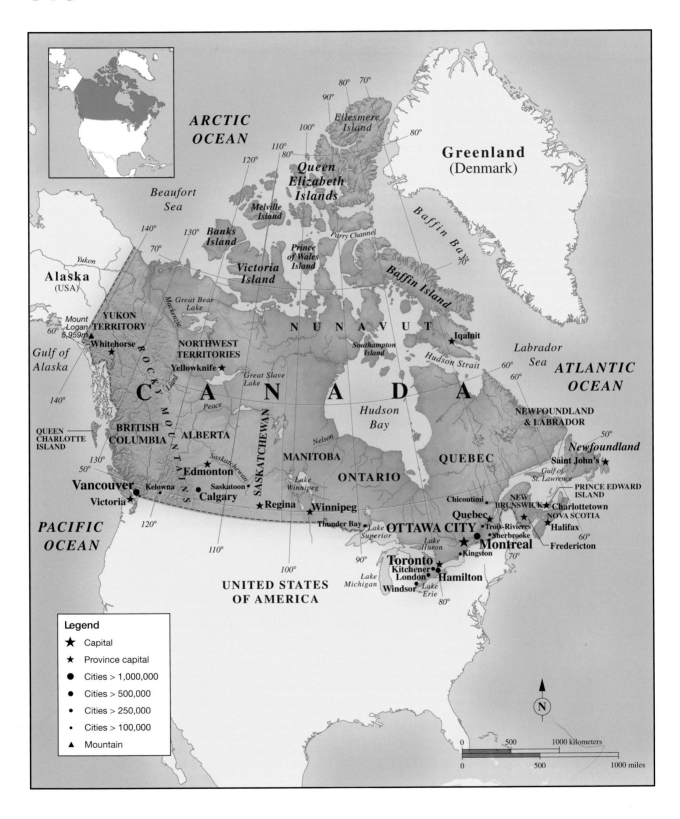

Legend

★ Capital

☆ Province capital

● Cities > 1,000,000

• Cities > 500,000

• Cities > 250,000

· Cities > 100,000

▲ Mountain

CHAPTER 2

History

The Inuit and North American Indians settled the part of North America that is now Canada between twenty-five thousand and thirty thousand years ago. Originally from Siberia and Mongolia, these first colonizers are thought to have crossed a land bridge connecting Asia and North America at that time. Some of them then moved eastward onto the Plains and south across the remainder of the North American continent.

Ancestors of today's Inuit people lived very frugally, hunting and fishing in the frozen north. Meanwhile, the Pacific Coast Indians, with access to abundant supplies of fish, woodland animals, furs, and timber, developed distinctive art forms, including totem poles and paintings. The Cree, Assiniboine, and Blackfoot groups of the Plains were nomadic peoples and hunted buffalo, using the meat for food and the hides to make clothing and tepees. Further east, the Algonquin and the Iroquois settled near the St. Lawrence River and grew crops such as maize, beans, and squash.

EUROPEAN EXPLORERS

Vikings landed on Canadian shores over one thousand years ago. These early explorers set up temporary settlements, using them as bases to collect timber and other resources to export to Greenland and Scandinavia. By about 1410, however, after enduring the extreme cold, disease, and battles with local tribes, the Vikings had abandoned all hope of

▼ A painting of John Cabot's ship, the *Matthew*, leaving Bristol, England, in 1497. Cabot's journey to Canada was one of many voyages that took place during the Age of Exploration, as European powers sought riches in distant lands.

▶ Canada's wilderness provided a rich supply of high-quality pelts, and many early settlers were fur trappers. They lived in simple log cabins, such as the one depicted in this scene.

permanent settlement in this hostile land. Later, after the success of Columbus's voyage to North America, other Europeans sailed the Atlantic in search of a new route to the spices and treasures of the Orient. In 1497, John Cabot, an Italian navigator, was given permission by Henry VII of England to sail west in search of bounty. Cabot landed on Cape Breton Island, off Newfoundland, but found no treasure or spices—only fish and trees. Nevertheless, fishers from England, France, Portugal, and Spain sailed there to harvest the plentiful cod.

Later, in the 1600s, European settlers were attracted to the area by its abundant furs. British and French fur-trappers flocked to this new land but clashed with the indigenous people. The Europeans, however, soon realized that they needed to trade with and gain knowledge from their new enemies.

Focus on: The French and the British

A French explorer, Simon de Champlain, formed an alliance with the Huron tribe, which was the traditional enemy of the Iroquois. This heightened the tension between the tribes. On one occasion, about three hundred Mohawk, who were allies of the Iroquois, were massacred by de Champlain's forces and the Huron. After this battle, the Iroquois joined forces with the Dutch and British. During the seventeenth and eighteenth centuries, there were frequent disputes between the French, the British, and the indigenous peoples. The French colony was at the heart of a struggle between the French and the British for supremacy in North America. In 1713, under the Treaty of Utrecht, Britain gained large areas of eastern Canada, including the valuable Hudson Bay and lands south of the Great Lakes. Later, in 1756, France and Britain began what became known as the French and Indian War. In 1763, the British army triumphed over France and its indigenous allies, and France surrendered all of its North American territories to Britain.

BIRTH OF A NEW COUNTRY

Until 1867, Canada was a collection of separate British-owned colonies. The people of these colonies were a mixture of British, French, and other recent settlers, along with the original indigenous Canadians. These separate colonies developed their own economies, mainly based on trading and utilizing the local natural resources. Apart from these settlements, the areas that remained virtually uninhabited in the middle of the nineteenth century included present-day Yukon, the Prairie Provinces, and parts of the Northwest Territories (most of which were still under the control of the British-owned Hudson's Bay Company).

VICTORIA, VANCOUVER'S ISLAND.

 This nineteenth-century engraving shows a small steamship anchored near Victoria, on Vancouver Island. In 1843, a Hudson's Bay Company post, Fort Camosun, was founded on the site of Victoria. In 1851, the city of Victoria was established as the capital of the crown colony of Vancouver Island. It became the capital of British Columbia in 1871.

Did You Know?
While sailing up the St. Lawrence River in 1534, Jacques Cartier, a French explorer, is said to have noticed that the First Nations people referred to their settlements as *kanata*, and he assumed that this was their name for the entire country. "Kanata" may have been an early version of "Canada."

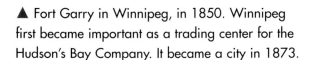

▲ Fort Garry in Winnipeg, in 1850. Winnipeg first became important as a trading center for the Hudson's Bay Company. It became a city in 1873.

During the United States Civil War (1861–1865), many people in the divided Canadian colonies feared that the United States might expand northward and take over valuable land in the Prairies. This perceived threat prompted the three key Canadian politicians of the period—George Cartier, John A. MacDonald, and George Brown—to unite Canada as a confederation in 1867. Nova Scotia, New Brunswick, and Canada (present-day Ontario and Quebec) were united under the British North American Act. Then, in 1868, the new Canadian government bought Rupert's Land from the Hudson's Bay Company. This agreement brought Manitoba into the confederation, followed by British Columbia (1871), Prince Edward Island (1873), Alberta and Saskatchewan (1905), and, finally, Newfoundland (1949).

Settling and uniting this vast new land was difficult. Regions that were rich in resources and close to rivers and ports, such as those along the St. Lawrence River, developed quickly. Inhospitable regions, such as the Yukon territories, were less attractive to settlers. In attempting to control and develop these more remote regions, the Canadian government often ignored the rights of the First Nations peoples. For instance, the agreement to purchase Rupert's Land from the Hudson's Bay Company took no account of the indigenous groups occupying the area. Among these groups were five thousand Metis Indians (the mixed-race French-speaking Catholic offspring of aboriginal and early European settlers) who had considered the land theirs for centuries.

Some land disputes between the Canadian government and First Nations peoples were settled in the twentieth century. One of the most significant settlements took place in 1992 and eventually led to the creation of Nunavut Territory in 1999. But many other land disputes are still being contested.

 Did You Know?

The Hudson's Bay Company was established in 1670, when King Charles II of England granted the company trapping and mineral rights over the land draining into the Hudson Bay, known as Rupert's Land. The company mainly used the port of York City to export fur pelts to Europe. The North American Fur Auction Company, the direct descendant of the Hudson's Bay Company, still exports furs all over the world.

▲ Nineteenth-century railroad workers stand with a locomotive belonging to the Canadian Pacific Railway, the first transcontinental transport link.

EARLY SETTLERS

The great Canadian Pacific Railway, built in 1869, helped link the parts of the confederation. Between 1896 and 1913, over one million people used it to reach unsettled land in the Prairies, or the area bounded to the west by the Rocky Mountains and to the east by Ontario including Alberta, Saskatchewan, and Manitoba.

Canadian government officials went to Europe to recruit settlers. Early migrants to the Prairies were offered 160 acres (65 hectares) of free land and Canadian citizenship, in exchange for a $10 registration fee and an agreement to stay on the land for at least six months of the year for three years in a row. Many of these settlers left Europe to escape economic depression and looked forward to making a fresh start in Canada. But few were prepared for the loneliness of prairie life and the extreme Canadian climate, with its hot dry summers and winter blizzards. Settlers, however, flooded into the Prairies, leading to an economic boom in places like Calgary and Vancouver. In 1896, gold was found in the Klondike, a river valley in the Yukon Territory. Over the next fifteen years, around thirty thousand people went there, hoping to make their fortunes, but few settled permanently.

TWENTIETH-CENTURY CHANGES

During World War I (1914-1918), Canadian soldiers fought alongside British troops against the Germans. The 1917 battle of Vimy Ridge in France was a notable victory for Canadian soldiers, even though it cost over eleven thousand Canadian lives. During World War I, Canadian wheat was in great demand in Europe because cheaper supplies from Russia were unavailable. After the war, however, Canada again competed as a wheat producer with Russia, Australia, and Argentina. To make things harder, the Prairie Provinces, Canada's main wheat-growing areas, were hit by droughts during this period, and harvests were poor. In addition, grain prices fell during the 1930s, and a deep depression hit the Canadian economy.

In 1931, the Statute of Westminster finally made Canada an autonomous state within the British Empire. This removed the last imperial power Britain had over Canada, meaning that it could no longer make laws for Canada unless it was asked. Newfoundland did not adopt the statute and remained under British rule until 1949, when it became a province of Canada.

In the World War II (1939–1945), Canadian soldiers joined the Allied forces (including Britain and the United States). After the war, the Canadian economy began to recover and the country again attracted immigrants. In the twentieth and twenty-first centuries, Canada has taken a leading role in international organizations, such as the North Atlantic Treaty Organization (NATO), a defensive alliance of North Atlantic countries formed in 1949, and the United Nations (UN). Canadian troops also served with the U.S.-led international coalition that liberated Afghanistan in 2001.

▲ A Canadian trooper prepares his gear near a Coyote reconnaissance vehicle at the Edmonton Garrison in January 2002, while getting ready for deployment in Afghanistan.

CHAPTER 3

Landscape and Climate

Large parts of Canada can be described as wilderness. The interior lowlands around Hudson Bay are said to make up around one-twelfth of the Earth's land surface and 80 percent of Canada's land area. The central feature of these lowlands is the Canadian Shield, a remnant of some immense granite mountains formed over 500 million years ago. The top layers of these mountains were scraped off by glaciers about seventy thousand years ago. The huge 10-foot (3-m) thick glaciers created a saucer-shaped depression, and this depression became Hudson Bay. Some of Canada's best farmland is in these lowland areas, which include the Prairie Provinces.

LAKES, RIVERS, AND MOUNTAINS

The Canada/United States border runs through the five famous Great Lakes of North America, allowing Canada and the United States to share them. Lakes Erie and Ontario are linked to the Atlantic Ocean by the 90 mile (145 km) long St. Lawrence Seaway. The St. Lawrence, the Mackenzie, the Yukon, and the Nelson-Saskatchewan are each among the forty longest rivers in the world.

▼ Snow-topped Rocky Mountain peaks, near Kicking Horse Pass, in Golden, British Columbia.

In western Canada, the Canadian Rocky Mountains extend through the Yukon Territory and British Columbia, occupying about 13 percent of Canada's land area. They dwarf the country's other mountains to the east (a northern extension of the Appalachian range). The Rocky Mountains started forming over 200 million years ago, when two vast sections of Earth's crust collided with each other and were forced up into a series of huge folds. Since then, glaciers have carved out the classic "dog-tooth" peaks. The Rockies extend approximately 3,000 miles (4,800 km), from Alaska in the north, through Canada and the United States, to Mexico in the south.

▼ Niagara Falls straddles the border between the United States and Canada and is the most visited waterfall in the world. The craft in this picture is approaching the Canadian side of the falls.

FROZEN LANDS

Nunavut and the Northwest Territories, in sub-Arctic northern Canada, are covered with ice during the extended winter, when temperatures can drop to below -60 °F (-51 °C). Temperatures are so low for most of the year that the subsurface remains permanently frozen, forming a layer called permafrost. The thin surface ice melts during the short summer, but the permafrost prevents water from draining away, and the landscape turns into a series of vast swamps, rivers, and lakes.

 Did You Know?

Niagara Falls is actually two waterfalls. The American Falls are 182 feet (55.5 m) high and 1,076 feet (328 m) wide. The Canadian Falls, known as Horseshoe Falls, are 177 feet (54 m) high and 2,200 feet (640 m) wide.

EXTREMES OF CLIMATE

Canada extends through more than forty-five degrees of latitude. Its surrounding oceans and highest mountain ranges affect its climate, often causing extreme weather patterns. Far northern Canada, for example, has Arctic conditions nearly all year round, falling to temperatures of -58 °F (-50 °C) in winter and receiving an average of 16 inches (41 centimeters) of snow. In contrast, summer temperatures in Vancouver often reach 86 °F (30 °C) and onshore winds blowing from the Pacific bring up to 60 inches (152 cm) of rainfall in a year.

British Columbia, on Canada's west coast, has the most temperate climate in the country, which encourages the growth of its extensive temperate rain forests. Warm westerly air blows in from the Pacific Ocean and cools as it is forced to ascend the western slopes of the Coastal Ranges and Rocky Mountains, causing heavy rainfall and snow. Further inland, the Prairies have a humid climate, with rainy springs, hot summers, and cold winters, that is ideal for growing grain.

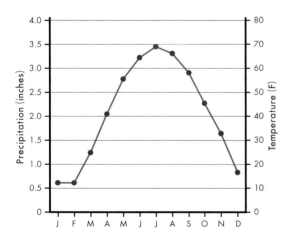

▲ Average monthly climate conditions in Ottawa

The St. Lawrence region, north of the Prairies and the Great Lakes, is snow-covered for much of the year. Moving toward the North Pole, the summer season gets shorter and winters get longer, with fewer hours of daylight to warm the atmosphere. In the far north, there is no real daylight at all when the overhead sun is positioned at its furthest point south over the Southern Hemisphere. This darkness may last about six weeks, with the amount of light increasing as the spring season approaches.

▲ Wheat fields in Saskatchewan. These flat plains are particularly prone to tornadoes, and Canada experiences approximately eighty tornadoes a year. One of the worst was the Pine Lake tornado, in Alberta, which killed eleven people in July 2000.

The area east of the Great Lakes-St. Lawrence region, on the Atlantic coast, has Canada's most variable climate. Influenced by air masses passing over the warm Gulf Stream ocean current and the occasional blast of cold air from the Arctic regions, St. John's, in Newfoundland, experiences temperatures as low as 23 °F (-5 °C) in winter and average highs of 68 °F (20 °C) in summer. Meanwhile, Toronto and Montreal, also in this eastern region but sheltered from the cooling effects of the oceans, have summer temperature averages of over 77 °F (25 °C).

 Did You Know?

The permanently white frozen snow cover in northern Canada reflects much of the sun's light energy back into the atmosphere, which reduces the amount of solar radiation, or heat, received. This is called the albedo effect.

Focus on: Climate Change

Canada's frozen wilderness areas are experiencing a number of problems, which many scientists believe are due to the effects of climate change caused by global warming. For example, on the islands of the Northwest Territories in the Beaufort Sea, ice sheets are thinning and becoming unsafe for travel, beaches are turning to mud, the permafrost is melting, and more thunderstorms are occurring (possibly due to the warming of the oceans). The local Inuit communities, who have learned over centuries to live in extremely cold temperatures, are finding it difficult to cope with these new and unpredictable weather patterns. Wildlife is also changing in these places. Species that are common in warmer climates, such as barn owls, geese, ducks, and salmon, are now appearing in Canada's frozen north. The number of polar bears, however, is declining because spring is coming earlier and fall later. This change causes shorter periods of ice cover and, therefore, less time for the bears to hunt seals, their main source of food. The polar bears' long-term survival is seriously threatened. Traditional Inuit culture, which is based on hunting polar bears and other animals that depend on the more extreme cold of the Arctic lands, is also at risk.

▼ A young adult polar bear on a field of melting ice in the Northwest Territories.

CHAPTER 4

Population and Settlements

Although Canada is the second-largest country in the world in terms of area, it has a relatively small population—only about thirty-two million—and one of the world's lowest population densities, with an average of 8.2 people per sq mile (3.2 people per sq km). Canada's population is also very unevenly distributed, with more than 65 percent of Canadians living on the 5 percent of the country's land that is taken up by the Great Lakes-St. Lawrence lowlands.

A MULTIETHNIC MOSAIC

Today's Canadians reflect the pattern of settlement over the past twenty-five thousand years. The early Inuit and native Indian, or First Nations, people were the original settlers, followed by Europeans (mainly British and French). More recently, a growing number of Asian people have been starting new lives in Canada. Just over 59 percent of Canadians speak English as their first language, 23.2 percent use French, and 17.5 percent use a variety of other languages. The early rivalries between the first French and British settlers are still evident in modern Canada. For instance, Quebec retains elements of French culture and identity, unlike the rest of the country.

In 1867, the newly formed government encouraged new settlers to occupy the vast open spaces of the empty country. By 1914, Canada had a population of eight million, three million of whom were immigrants from Europe. Today, 15 percent of Canadians were born in another country, and immigration is still encouraged to

Population Data

- 📂 Population: 31.7 million
- 📂 Population 0–14 yrs: 18%
- 📂 Population 15–64 yrs: 69%
- 📂 Population 65+ yrs: 13%
- 📂 Population growth rate (2000–2005): 0.8%
- 📂 Population density: 8.2 per sq mile/ 3.2 per sq km
- 📂 Urban population: 80%
- 📂 Major cities:
  Montreal 3,511,000
  Ottawa 1,120,000
  Toronto 5,060,000
  Vancouver 2,125,000

Sources: United Nations and World Bank

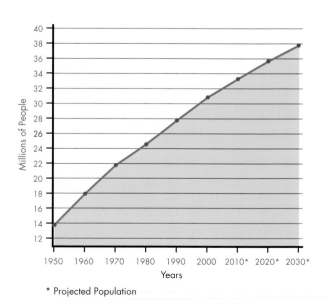

* Projected Population

▲ Population growth, 1950–2030

some extent. Most of Canada's recent immigrants come from China, as shown by the growth of large Chinatown districts in Canada's cities. For instance, Chinatown in Vancouver is home to over one hundred thousand Chinese people and is the second-largest Chinese community outside East Asia. (San Francisco has an even larger Chinese population.)

▲ This store in Vancouver sells Chinese goods. The city has a large Chinese population.

Focus on: Chinese Boat People

There has been growing concern in Canada, particularly in British Columbia, about the number of Chinese "boat people" arriving in the country. Many of these immigrants, who claim refugee status, arrive in poorly maintained ships that are only capable of making a one-way journey. Many of them have also used their life savings to pay people-smugglers, known as "snakeheads," who charge high prices to arrange their illegal journeys. It is estimated that 70 percent of those claiming to be refugees fail to follow the official procedures for immigrants, and "disappear" into the close-knit Chinese communities. Canada is a growing economy and needs more workers, but many Canadians feel immigration controls should be stricter. They welcome a diverse culture but see the need to tighten rules on illegal trafficking of people.

FIRST NATIONS PEOPLE

Many First Nations people have become integrated into modern Canadian society. Some, however, have found it difficult to adjust to the loss of their traditional, rural way of life. In large cities, such as Toronto and Montreal, some First Nations people have found themselves among the most disadvantaged groups in society. Several First Nations groups now live in government-built reservations, and some of them suffer problems linked to crime, alcoholism, and drugs.

Many First Nations people have protested to the government about the way it mistreated their people in the past by taking their land and using them as cheap yet highly skilled labor. (The First Nations people's understanding of their environment was essential to the success of many early enterprises, such as fur trapping.) In 1998, the Canadian government formally apologized for its past mistreatment of the country's native peoples. The government is now making efforts to support First Nations people who are working to preserve their heritage. For instance, Nunavut, with a mainly Inuit population of only twenty-five thousand, was made a separate territory in 1999, according to the principle of "aboriginal title," under which ancestral lands are being returned to First Nations people.

The Haida people, who are from the Queen Charlotte Islands, have also regained control of their land. When Europeans first arrived on these islands, in 1774, the Haida population was over ten thousand. Today, they number about six thousand. Since the Haida Nation won a landmark case in Canada's Supreme Court, the British Columbian government has had to consult with the Haida people over land use on their traditional homelands on the Queen Charlotte Islands.

▼ Haida people at a canoe dedication ceremony at Skidegate, on Graham Island, in the Queen Charlotte Islands, British Columbia.

 Did You Know?

Inuit people rejected the name by which they were commonly known, *Eskimo*, because it means "eater of meat" and was used by the Algonquin natives as an insult. The word *Inuit* means "person."

CITY LIFE

Around 73 percent of Canada's population lives in urban settlements, mostly within 93 miles (150 km) of the United States border. Outside this narrow corridor, limited road and rail access has restricted the growth of settlements to a few small isolated towns and tourist or regional centers such as Whitehorse, Yukon's capital (population 19,058). All Canada's large cities have direct access to the Atlantic or Pacific Oceans, either by canal or by the St. Lawrence Seaway, and most have thriving ports.

The country's largest city, Toronto (population 4,551,800), is located on the northern shore of Lake Ontario. Toronto is very similar to many large cities in the United States, with streets laid out in a grid pattern and a busy downtown business area surrounded by low-rise sprawling suburbs.

Canada's capital is Ottawa (population 863,000), in the province of Ontario. Often considered rather dull compared with Toronto and Montreal, Ottawa is in fact a vibrant center that hosts more festivals than any other Canadian city. During the harsh winters, the Rideau Canal running through the city freezes solid, and many commuters skate to work.

▲ A night photograph of Toronto's downtown skyline, showing Lake Ontario in the foreground.

Quebec City (population 643,200) was the original capital of French Canada. It is overshadowed today, however, by Montreal (population 3,256,300), located on an island in the St. Lawrence Seaway. Montreal is the second-largest city in Canada, the world's largest French-speaking city outside France, and the site of more historic buildings than any other city in North America. Montreal, however, experiences subzero winter temperatures and very hot, humid summers.

Canada's third-largest city, Vancouver (population 1,836,500), is the country's only major city on the Pacific coast of the mainland. As the economies of China and Southeast Asia expand, Vancouver is becoming increasingly important in Canada's economic growth.

 Did You Know?

The UN rates Canada as one of the best countries in which to live. Canada's life expectancy and standard of education rank among the highest in the world.

CHAPTER 5

Government and Politics

Canada is a confederation of seven provinces and three territories. The Oregon Treaty of 1846 fixed the forty-ninth parallel as the boundary between the continental United States and Canada. The Canadian coat of arms includes the lion, the unicorn, the British flag, and the fleur-de-lis, reflecting Canada's strong historical links with Britain and France.

FEDERAL AND PROVINCIAL GOVERNMENT

Canada is a federal multiparty democracy, with each province voting in its own regional party and an overall majority governing the country. Canada has six political parties, and the Liberal Party has been the governing party since 1993. Prime Minister Paul Martin succeeded Jean Chrétien in December 2003 and was reelected in June 2004 to serve the next five years in office. The country has a bicameral parliament, which means that its legislature has two houses. The senate has 105 members, appointed by the governor general; the House of Commons has 301 members, who are elected by the public.

Canada is such a large country, with so many different cultures, that the question of whether certain provinces, particularly Quebec and British Columbia, should have their own separate autonomous governments, has been debated many times. Each provincial government is responsible for local taxation, spending, and laws concerning social issues, while laws drawn up by the federal government apply nationwide. Each province has powers to pass laws within its own borders, but it cannot pass an act to change its membership in the confederation of Canada.

◀ Canadian prime minister Paul Martin (left) stands with United States president George W. Bush during the Summit of the Americas in Monterrey, Mexico, in 2004. Leaders of thirty-four nations met here to discuss regional issues, including economic policies.

CANADA'S PRIME MINISTERS

Canada's political system, modeled on the British style of government, has a prime minister at its head. The title "prime minister" comes from the Latin phrase *primus inter pares,* meaning "first among equals." The prime minister is the leader, or first among equals, in the government cabinet of ministers and first among the people of the country.

Canada has had twenty-one prime ministers since 1867, beginning with John Alexander MacDonald, who served for six years. The longest-serving prime minister was Pierre Trudeau, who stayed in office a total of over fifteen years—for two consecutive terms, from 1968 to 1979, and from 1980 to 1984. Not all Canada's prime ministers have served their full term of office, and Canada's only woman prime minister, Kim Campbell, served only between June and November 1993.

Only two of Canada's prime ministers, John Alexander MacDonald (1878–1891) and John Sparrow David Thompson (1892–1894), have died in office. Others have retired from office or have served as opposition leaders after their party was voted out of office.

Focus on: Self-government by Indigenous Peoples

In 1999, the territory of Nunavut was created on land that was formerly part of the Northwest Territories. This new state was founded by the Canadian government partly as a way of compensating for previous mistreatment of Inuit communities. There are about fifty thousand Inuit people in the north, and Nunavut is the first state in modern history to be governed by indigenous Canadians. In addition, since the late 1970s, Inuit people along the Labrador coast have been campaigning to claim control over their ancestral lands, which are part of a sparsely populated area covering over 27,992 sq miles (72,500 sq km).

◀ Assembly of First Nations chief Phil Fontaine (left), who is Anishinabe (Ojibwe or Chippewa) from Sagkeeng First Nation in Manitoba, meets Ottawa government ministers in 2004 to discuss problems with the health-care system.

▲ In 1995, a crowd of 150,000 Canadians rallied in Montreal against the separation of Quebec from the rest of Canada. Many in the crowd waved Canadian flags.

INDEPENDENCE FOR QUEBEC?

Conflict between French and British Canadians began in 1759, when the British won the battle for supremacy in North America on the Plains of Abraham just outside Quebec City. At this point, Quebec was formally granted to Britain and made part of British North America. Over the next two hundred years, conflict between the British and French in Quebec persisted. When Canada became a confederation in 1867, the province of Quebec was established, with both English and French as its official languages.

During the 1960s, there was a growing movement, led by artists, writers, and politicians—including then-prime minister Pierre Trudeau—in favor of Quebec separating from the rest of Canada. A separatist political party, the Parti Quebecois (PQ), was formed in 1968. The PQ gained control of Quebec's provincial government and made French the official language of the province in 1976.

 Did You Know?

The slogan of separatist campaigners—"Vive Le Quebec Libre!," which means "Long Live Free Quebec"—came from the French president Charles de Gaulle when he visited Quebec in 1967.

Since the PQ came to power, the previous dominance of Anglophone (English-speaking) people in Quebec's government, its civil service, and its businesses has been reversed, in favor of Francophones (French-speakers). Many new Francophone businesses were set up through a project called Quebec Inc., which supported French-speaking businessmen. Higher education opportunities for Francophones were also expanded. Quebec now has four French-language and three English-language universities. In addition, French Canadians in Quebec earn slightly more on average than English Canadians in the province. At the same time, many English-speaking businesses have left Montreal and Quebec and moved to Toronto. This has caused some unemployment in Quebec and has increased the need to attract more industry to the province.

? Did You Know?

Public signs in Quebec have to be in French and English. On many unofficial signs, however, there is no English at all.

The PQ has continued to strive for Quebec's independence from the other provinces of Canada. Although the PQ is now the party in power in Quebec, the province is still part of Canada. The people of Quebec have been given two opportunities to vote on this issue. The last vote was in 1995, and separation was narrowly rejected.

▲ All signs in the province of Quebec appear in both French and English. Many of the French-speaking people of Quebec would like Quebec to become independent from Canada.

CHAPTER 6

Energy and Resources

Canada is one of the most resource-rich countries in the world, and it was the fifth-largest energy producer in 2001 (after the United States, Russia, China, and Saudi Arabia). Energy production is Canada's second-largest industry, and it includes uranium, used in the production of nuclear power; fossil fuels such as oil, coal, and natural gas; and hydroelectric power (HEP).

▲ Massive machinery scoops up black tar sands in a huge open-cast mine in Athabasca. Oil will be extracted from these tar sands.

Energy Data

- Energy consumption as % of world total: 2.8
- Energy consumption by sector (% of total):
  - Industry: 40
  - Transportation: 29
  - Agriculture: 2
  - Services: 13
  - Residential: 16
- CO_2 emissions as % of world total: 2.1
- CO_2 emissions per capita in tons per year: 17.6

Source: World Resources Institute

Focus on: Oil Sands

In the isolated Fort McMurray area, on the Athabasca River, northern Alberta, there is a reserve of some 4,478 sq miles (11,600 sq km) of sticky, black, bituminous oil sands. Amid growing fears of diminishing oil reserves, rising prices, and possible disruption of supplies from the Middle East owing to political instability, the oil sands of the Athabasca may possibly offer a secure, affordable oil supply for North America. The crude oil extracted from the Athabasca oil sands, however, is much thicker than conventionally drilled oil. Because of its thickness, it is more expensive to transport and refine. It is also difficult to get people to work in such inhospitable wilderness areas without paying high wages. Furthermore, the refining process produces far higher levels of CO_2, which will make it difficult for Canada to reduce its emissions in line with the targets set at the Earth Summit in Kyoto, Japan, in 1997. The Canadian oil company, Petro-Canada, is searching for ways around these problems, but the environmental and financial costs of securing long-term oil supplies from the sands of Athabasca could turn out to be very high.

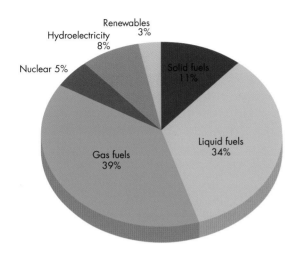

▲ Energy use by type

Renewables 3%
Hydroelectricity 8%
Nuclear 5%
Solid fuels 11%
Liquid fuels 34%
Gas fuels 39%

ENERGY PRODUCTION

Canada has huge natural gas reserves and is the world's third-largest producer, providing about 87 percent of the U.S. natural gas supply. Coal is also an important export for Canada, with much of the coal it produces going to Japan and South Korea. Canada's proven oil reserves in 2004 were 197 billion tons (179 billion metrics tons)—one of the world's largest reserves. Most of the oil is produced in Alberta and the western provinces, but most is consumed in Ontario and the eastern provinces.

Canada is also one of the world's largest producers of hydroelectric power (HEP), and this form of electricity supplies 61 percent of the country's needs. Quebec and Ontario produce most of their HEP from their fast-flowing rivers. Use of HEP, however, has caused some concern about Quebec's environment. Many forest areas have been cleared, and land has been flooded, in the process of constructing large dams for HEP programs. In addition, much of this land was previously occupied by First Nations people, who were forced to leave.

About 21 percent of Canada's electricity is generated by fossil-fuel power stations that use coal, oil, and gas, and nuclear energy provides 17 percent. Eager to meet its Kyoto target (a 6 percent reduction of its CO_2 emissions by 2010), Canada is trying to develop renewable forms of energy, such as wind power, which uses turbines to convert the wind's energy into electricity. Another renewable form of energy involves photovoltaic (PV) cells, which can be mounted in solar panels to convert the energy of the sun into electricity. Even though solar and wind power produce only 1 percent of Canada's electricity at present, they are particularly well suited to isolated communities, where the cost of connection to the national grid is high.

▼ Revelstoke Dam, on the Columbia River, is one of many large dams that have been built in Canada to generate hydroelectric power (HEP).

ENERGY CONSUMPTION

Many Canadians drive powerful vehicles that use large amounts of fuel. They need to keep warm in the extremely cold winters and cool in the often humid, hot summers. All these requirements add up to heavy energy consumption. In fact, Canada is the eighth-largest energy consumer in the world.

As Canada is so rich in energy resources, it exports over 31 percent of what it produces to the United States, mainly in the form of electricity. The importance of the energy link between the two countries was clearly demonstrated in August 2003, when power cuts in the Great Lakes-Ontario area and the northeastern states of the United States caused a major disruption. Apparently, a very high demand from air-conditioning units in northern Ohio during this hot August period overloaded grid supply lines, resulting in a shut-down of supply in the wider region.

MINERALS AND OTHER RESOURCES

Canada also has abundant deposits of metal ores and minerals. During the 1890s, there was a gold rush in the Yukon and British Columbia, and thousands of people from all over the world came to the region's Klondike area. Today, Canada is known as the world's largest producer of zinc and the second-largest producer of nickel. Other ores, such as copper, potash, asbestos, gypsum, and coltan (used in the manufacture of circuit boards), are also mined in the country. In addition, Canada is the world's largest exporter of timber products and wheat, and Canada's oceans, lakes, and wildernesses hold vast numbers of fish and animals with fur pelts.

◄ Highland Valley Copper Mine, in the Rocky Mountains, is one of the world's largest copper mines, processing 39,200 tons (35,560 metric tons) of copper a day.

TIMBER PRODUCTION

Around 50 percent of Canada is covered in forest. The coniferous forests of the north make up approximately 80 percent of Canada's total forests. The remainder consists of old-growth rain forests on the west coast of British Columbia and Vancouver Island and the deciduous forests of the east.

Focus on: Rain Forest of the North

The Pacific temperate rain forest on Vancouver Island, off the west coast of British Columbia, produces ten times more wood than the South American rain forest. The huge trees in this forest—including Sitka spruce, cedar, spruce, and Douglas fir—are very valuable. A single Sitka trunk can fetch up to $60,000.

This rain forest once stretched from Alaska to northern California. Deforestation is a major environmental problem in Canada, especially in British Columbia and on Vancouver Island. The forests are being removed by clear-cutting, or clearing all the trees in an area and leaving the land exposed, which is particularly damaging to the environment. Important habitats are destroyed, and soils are left exposed to rainfall, causing serious soil erosion. Environmentalists try to raise public awareness of these issues.

▼ A female forester at work in a forest north of Nanaimo, on Vancouver Island.

CHAPTER 7

Economy and Income

Canada has a huge wealth of resources and a relatively low population to make use of them. This is partly why Canada is one of the most important trading nations in the world. It is also well located for trade with some of the world's strongest and fastest-growing economies, particularly the United States, China, and Southeast Asia.

IMPORTS AND EXPORTS

The Canadian dollar is weaker than the U.S. dollar, so Canada makes an attractive trading partner for the United States. Yet, despite the relative weakness of the Canadian dollar, the total value of Canada's exports is higher than its imports, giving it a trade surplus. Most of Canada's exports are raw materials, and the bulk of its imports are manufactured goods.

Economic Data

- Gross National Income (GNI) in U.S.$: 756,770,340,864
- World rank by GNI: 8
- GNI per capita in U.S.$: 23,930
- World rank by GNI per capita: 24
- Economic growth: 2%

Source: World Bank

In 1989, the United States, Canada, and Mexico formed the North Atlantic Free Trade Agreement (NAFTA). This agreement, which went into effect in 1994, allows the three countries to trade with each other without having to pay import or export taxes. NAFTA has led to a growth in trade for all three countries and a strong demand for Canadian products. It has also increased the volume of goods that Canada imports from Mexico and the United States. In 2004, Canada was Mexico's second-largest market for exports.

FORESTRY AND AGRICULTURE

Canada's forest products industry provides jobs for over one million Canadians, and it brings in fifty-five billion Canadian dollars annually. Two-thirds of this income comes from lumber, plywood, and wood products, and the remaining third from pulp and paper. About half the world's newspapers are produced using paper made from Canadian trees, and the country is the world's largest supplier of paper-grade pulp, exporting 80 percent of what it manufactures to over one hundred countries. The largest customer is the United States, followed by Japan, China, and Britain. As demand for printing paper increases, the

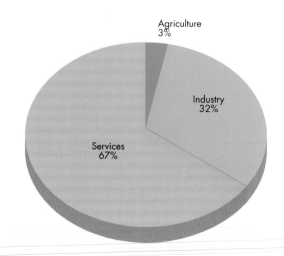

▲ Economy by sector

industry is responding by using more recycled paper. Around 75 percent of Canadian pulp is made of either recovered paper or wood chips and residue, which would previously have ended up in landfill sites. The process of making pulp involves either mechanically or chemically separating out wood fiber, and this uses large amounts of water and energy. The Forestry Products Association of Canada is working to promote more environmentally sensitive ways of managing the industry. For instance, it is decreasing the use of fossil fuels. It is also including more First Nations people in management partnerships.

Another small but nevertheless important sector of the Canadian economy is agriculture, which employs many people on farms and in related industries, such as transportation, processing, and the manufacturing and maintenance of farm equipment. Most of Canada's cultivated land lies within about 300 miles (500 km) of the U.S. border. Canadian farm products include livestock, fruit, tobacco, and potatoes, but Canada is probably best known for its grain crops. It is the second-largest exporter of grain in the world. Around 75 percent of the country's cultivated land is in the prairie regions, with Saskatchewan growing two-thirds of the country's wheat. Transport links are very important to this export industry. Trains take the grain westward to Vancouver for export to the Japanese and East Asian markets and eastward to Churchill, on the Hudson Bay, or Thunder Bay, on Lake Superior, for export to the European markets.

▼ Grain is emptied from a tractor-driven combine into a trailer during the harvesting of a wheat field in Ebenezar, Saskatchewan.

Focus on: The Fishing Industry

Canada's fishing industry was worth more than $5 billion a year in 2002, and it exports over 75 percent of its fish each year. The Atlantic catches provide 82 percent of the total, while 14 percent come from the Pacific fisheries, and 4 percent come from freshwater sources. Atlantic lobsters are Canada's most valuable seafood product, and hake, salmon, clams, and halibut are also important. In the mid-1990s, a ban was imposed on fishing cod off the Atlantic Grand Banks because of falling fish stocks. This ban encouraged the growth of fish farming, or aquaculture, which accounted for 14 percent of Canada's total fish production in 2002. There are, however, growing concerns about the environmental impact of fish farms. Farmed salmon are often kept in open net cages in the sea, and excess food and organic waste from the fish farms pollute the ocean bed.

▲ A worker harvests salmon by netting them from a pen on a fish farm in British Columbia.

MANUFACTURING AND SERVICE INDUSTRIES

Around 67 percent of Canada's gross domestic income is generated by service industries and 32 percent by manufacturing. The main manufacturing industries in Canada are timber, pulp, and paper processing; chemicals; and

▲ A pulp mill at Alberni, on Vancouver Island. These mills require massive volumes of water to manufacture pulp.

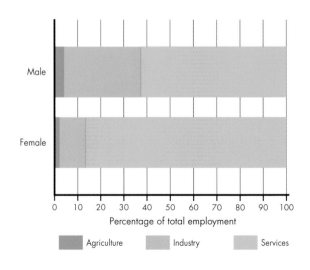

Percentage of total employment

▬ Agriculture   ▬ Industry   ▬ Services

▲ Labor force by sector and gender

▶ A finishing mill operator sits at the control panel at Algoma Steel Mill, in Ontario. Thick steel blocks are reheated to a nearly molten state before they are run at high speed through a series of mills. The heated steel is the bright orange band that can be seen through the control room windows.

metals. The provinces of Ontario and Quebec, in the Great Lakes-St. Lawrence region, are Canada's major industrial areas. Cheap hydroelectric power, a large number of people, easy access to the United States, and transportation via the Great Lakes and St. Lawrence Seaway are all factors that have helped industry thrive in this region. Montreal is an important center for clothing manufacturing, and Toronto specializes in aircraft manufacturing. The country's automobile and truck industry is also located in this area, fed by the huge steel mills at Hamilton, commonly known as "Steel City," on the shores of Lake Ontario. Japanese and Southeast Asian companies

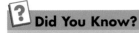

? Did You Know?

Canadians save more money per head and buy more insurance than the people of any other nation in the world. This provides plenty of business for their growing finance industry.

account for about 12 percent of investment in Canada's businesses. When foreign businesses expand in North America, however, many find Canadian production costs too high and set up in the United States or Mexico—where labor and production costs are lower—instead.

Centered in the major cities, one growing industry in Canada is financial services, such as banking and insurance. With many attractions and a large customer base, including both Canadians and visitors from abroad, tourism is another important industry in Canada. The tourist industry is well supported by the Canadian government. Canada's film industry is also growing fast, with Vancouver and Toronto both claiming the title "Hollywood North." Vancouver is an ideal location for American film companies, because it looks like a typical North American city. It has a mild climate all year, and it is far less expensive to film in than a location in the United States.

CHAPTER 8

Global Connections

As an important economic power in the world, Canada has been one of the G8 industrially developed democracies since 1976. Heads of government and major industrial leaders from these countries meet regularly to discuss a wide range of issues, including international trade regulation with developing countries, environmental questions, terrorism, and policies for regulating weapons and drugs.

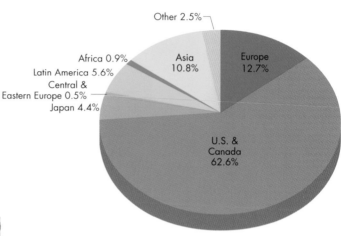

Other 2.5%
Africa 0.9%
Latin America 5.6%
Central & Eastern Europe 0.5%
Japan 4.4%
Asia 10.8%
Europe 12.7%
U.S. & Canada 62.6%

▲ Origin of imports by major trading region

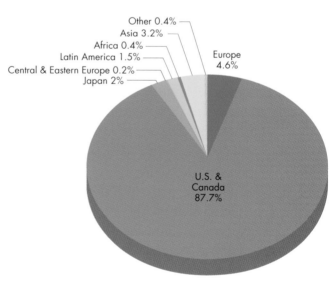

Other 0.4%
Asia 3.2%
Africa 0.4%
Latin America 1.5%
Central & Eastern Europe 0.2%
Japan 2%
Europe 4.6%
U.S. & Canada 87.7%

▲ Destination of exports by major trading region

◀ Canadian prime minister Paul Martin (left) meets United Nations secretary-general Kofi Annan at the United Nations headquarters, in New York, in 2004.

CANADA, BRITAIN, AND FRANCE

As a Commonwealth country, Canada retains strong links with Britain. The British queen, Elizabeth II, is the country's head of state, and the Canadian government is modeled on the British government and legislative system. Canada, however, no longer has any political allegiance to the British government. In 1982—in further recognition of Canada's independence—all powers relating to Canada in British law were ended. The links between Quebec and France are only through language, culture, and religion; there are no political ties.

CANADA AND THE UNITED STATES

The relationship between Canada and the United States is, on the whole, very friendly. Because countries sharing a border are affected by each other's actions, however, occasional disputes occur. Resource exploitation and pollution have been particular causes of contention. For example, Canadians have

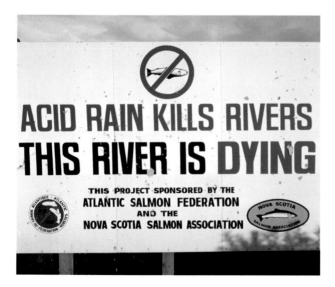

▲ Nova Scotia fishing organizations warn people of the danger of acid rain and the toxic effect it has had on a local river.

a long-standing dispute with some industries on the U.S. side of the border that pollute the atmosphere. Pollutants such as sulphur dioxide and nitrogen oxide mix with water vapor in the air to form an acidic solution known as acid rain, which damages Canadian forests. Oil spills and pollution from Alaskan pipelines and ports have also affected Canadian wildlife.

Canada and the United States cooperate closely on most defense issues. Canada was a founding member of the North Atlantic Treaty Organization (NATO), through which it pledges support for other NATO members in times of conflict. The country joined the United Nations (UN) in 1945, and Canadian soldiers have served in many conflicts as members of UN peacekeeping forces, including those in Afghanistan and in the former Yugoslavia. Eleven Canadians died in the terrorist attacks on the United States on September 11, 2001. Since then, the United States and Canada have been supporting each other in the war on terror, through increased vigilance along their 5,000 mile (8,000 km) border. Both countries have also increased security checks on people entering from the outside.

Nevertheless, the Canadian government did not support U.S. president George W. Bush's decision to invade Iraq in 2003. In recent years, all NATO members have been cutting back on defense spending and have been switching their efforts to rapid reaction, rather than long-term peace-keeping, strategies. Canada withdrew all its peacekeeping troops from European bases in 1992, and in 2004, Canada announced that it was calling many of its peacekeeping troops home. For example, Canadian troops made up one quarter of the UN peacekeeping force in Haiti,

which has suffered several coups. Now all those soldiers, along with troops from Bosnia and Afghanistan, are being recalled. Despite these cutbacks, the Canadian government remains committed to peace initiatives and is a leading campaigner against landmines. A treaty to ban their production, export, and use was formally ratified by 141 countries in Ottawa in 1997. Canada has also funded an aid package to train thirty thousand Iraqi police in the newly independent Iraq.

THE SCANDINAVIA OF NORTH AMERICA?

The Scandinavian countries are well known for their generous contributions to aid programs for developing countries. In the twentieth century, Canada also had a very good record as a donor country and was sometimes called the

▲ In this photograph, taken in 1994, a major in the Canadian armed forces walks with Rwandan children in Kigali who were displaced by the Rwandan civil war.

"Scandinavia of North America." In more recent years, however, Canada has not ranked among the top donor countries. For example, in 2003, Norwegians gave U.S.$307.95 per person in overseas development aid, compared with U.S.$40.36 per person from Canada. Canada was ranked twelfth out of twenty-two in the United Nations generosity league, and its aid donations continue to fall short of the UN aid target of 0.7 percent of its gross national product (GNP). Canada, however, made the fifth-largest pledge of government aid to the Tsunami Disaster Fund in January 2005, with a total of U.S.$340,644,000 (equal to U.S.$10.71 per person). The Canadian International Development Agency (CIDA) used to be heavily committed to aid programs in the Horn of Africa. Some of these projects were very successful, but other aid programs have been criticized for appearing to benefit Canadian manufacturers of machinery and materials more than the intended recipients of the aid.

The Wheat Project in Tanzania during the mid-1990s was a case in point. Areas farmed by the indigenous Barabaig cattle farmers were instead used to grow wheat on a large scale in an attempt to improve food supplies. This type of wheat farming, however, required expensive equipment. At first, this equipment was donated by Canadian firms. Additional or replacement equipment, however, had to be paid for by the Tanzanian government. Canadian agricultural machinery manufacturers benefited from the sales, while the Tanzanian government's debts

increased. Meanwhile, the cattle farmers had lost their land, and the wheat produced was too expensive for local people to buy.

CIDA now plans to concentrate its work in Africa on health and nutrition, basic education, treatment of HIV/AIDS, and protection of children. Nongovernmental organizations (NGOs), such as Canadian Oxfam, have been successful in African countries. Canada is now also directing more aid toward Asian and eastern European countries.

▲ An Afghan worker lifts a bag of wheat donated by a Canadian agency in Peshawar in 2001.

 Did You Know?

Voluntary aid programs show Canadian individuals to be very generous. In a 2004 appeal to help people suffering in the Darfur area of Sudan, the Canadian Auto Workers alone raised $150,000.

Focus on: CIVA

Canadian Village India (CIVA) is one of many nonprofit charitable organizations in Canada. Based in Vancouver, CIVA collaborates with agencies and organizations working in rural India, encouraging improvements in education and health care and campaigning on issues ranging from the rights of women and children to environmental concerns. For example, it began working in villages in the Kutch region after an earthquake in 2001, helping children gain access to education.

CHAPTER 9

Transportation and Communications

Distance has always been a major obstacle for people in Canada. The extreme climate and hostile landscape have made it almost impossible to build roads and railways in some areas. Much of the country north of the fiftieth parallel is covered by large lakes and swamps which freeze over during the long winters. Communities in remote areas largely depend on single-engine airplanes for contact with the outside world. Canada has 1,389 airports, although 886 of them have unpaved runways.

Transport & Communications Data

- Total roads: 874,915 miles/1,408,000 km
- Total paved roads: 308,827 miles/ 497,306 km
- Total unpaved roads: 565,541 miles/ 910,694 km
- Total railroads: 30,710 miles/49,422 km
- Major airports: 503
- Cars per 1,000 people: 458
- Cellular phones per 1,000 people: 377
- Personal computers per 1,000 people: 487
- Internet users per 1,000 people: 513

Sources: World Bank and CIA World Factbook

▼ A seaplane at Iconnu Lodge, Yukon Territory.

The recently opened Nunavut Arctic College has links with other Arctic-based colleges and provides the local Inuit people with access to higher education and life-long learning based on their own culture and traditional values. The Canadian government is also investing in improving access to computers and the Internet for First Nations communities.

▼ Students at the University of Toronto changing classes. Canada has a well-educated population and many world-class universities.

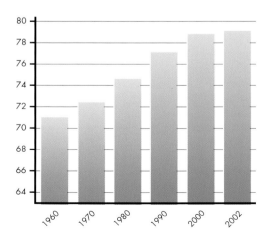

▲ Life expectancy at birth, 1960–2002

Education and Health Data

- ☞ Life expectancy at birth male: 76.2
- ☞ Life expectancy at birth female: 82.4
- ☞ Infant mortality rate per 1,000: 5
- ☞ Under-five mortality rate per 1,000: 7
- ☞ Physicians per 1,000 people: 2.1
- ☞ Health expenditure as % of GDP: 9.5
- ☞ Education expenditure as % of GDP: 5.2
- ☞ Primary school net enrollment %: 99
- ☞ Student-teacher ratio, primary: 17
- ☞ Adult literacy % age 15+: 99

Sources: United Nations Agencies and World Bank

HEALTH CARE AND HEALTH PROBLEMS

Canadian health care is funded by a national insurance system, and the government spends large amounts of money ensuring that its people enjoy one of the best health-care systems in the world. Hospitals and health centers in towns and cities are well equipped and there are plenty of doctors available to treat patients. It is harder to find doctors in more remote areas, however, where it is difficult to get doctors to fill vacant positions. The government is trying to attract more doctors to these areas by offering attractive pay packages with "isolation pay" or "hardship benefits."

Unfortunately, not all Canadians enjoy a high standard of living. A growing number suffer problems of poverty and deprivation, particularly those on low incomes. This group includes some indigenous people. Many First Nations people live on reservations, which often lack the basic services that most other Canadians take for granted. The Canadian government has recognized that there is a particular problem of child poverty and deprivation in reservation communities.

Nationally, Canada has an aging population. However, the First Nations communities, which make up just 4 percent of the country's population, have 7 percent of the country's children below the age of six. Many of these children face problems of poverty and ill health. The government has started to fund new community projects and provide more basic child-care and education programs in reservation areas, but there is still much to be

▼ Inuit children playing hockey in the Northwest Territories. Remote areas in Canada often have fewer health-care facilities than other places in the country.

done to improve the health and educational opportunities for these children.

As in other developed countries, such as the United States and Britain, some of the most common causes of death in modern Canada are cancer, strokes, heart disease, and respiratory disease. Despite Canada's excellent health record, a growing number of Canadians eat a lot of high-fat fast foods and do not exercise enough, leading to obesity and other health problems. In addition, the country has not escaped the global HIV/AIDS pandemic, with an estimated fifty thousand Canadians living with HIV/AIDS and five hundred recorded AIDS deaths in 2002. Many of those living with HIV are able to control their symptoms by taking medication. The government funds public education programs to combat HIV/AIDS, including regular Internet updates giving guidance on preventative measures.

In a country with higher than average car ownership in which many people do a lot of driving, it is not surprising that one of the major causes of death in Canada is road accidents. The rates vary from region to region, with the urban death rate being far lower than that in rural areas. The territory that has the highest number of road deaths by far is the Yukon Territory. Poor road conditions, long distances, extreme weather, and driver fatigue all contribute to the high number of accidents in this area.

 Did You Know?

For travelers to Canada, most of the major health hazards are associated with the outdoors. These hazards include giardia, or "beaver fever," which is caused by a parasite that is found in soil, food, hot springs, stagnant water, and streams. The symptoms include vomiting and stomach cramps.

Focus on: The SARS Outbreak

In April 2003, Toronto hit the world news, when Canada became the only country outside Asia to report cases of Severe Acute Respiratory Syndrome (SARS). The outbreak of the deadly virus had earlier been reported in Hong Kong, mainland China, and other Southeast Asian countries. The disease is thought to have been carried into Canada by a visitor from Asia. The Canadian Health Authority responded quickly by quarantining the infected patients and publishing fact sheets to inform the public and contain the spread of the disease. Meanwhile, the World Health Organization advised overseas business travelers and tourists to avoid going to Toronto. This warning lasted only a few weeks.

▲ A family arriving in Canada from China walks through Vancouver International Airport wearing masks, as fear of SARS spread to Canada.

CHAPTER 11

Culture and Religion

Life in many Canadian towns and cities is similar to life in the United States and Britain. All the same big-name stores and restaurants line the city streets. There are designer clothes shops, movie theaters, music festivals, museums, art galleries, and sports arenas. Canadians enjoy a wide range of culture and entertainment.

A RICH CULTURAL LIFE

Toronto's theaters are surpassed only by those of London and New York. Well-known Canadian actors include Michael J. Fox and Donald Sutherland. Popular Canadian musical performers, such as Celine Dion, Neil Young, Leonard Cohen, Joni Mitchell, Rush, and Sarah McLachlan, have also become famous all over the world. This rich culture has emerged in large cities such as Toronto and Vancouver, where different ethnic groups, including immigrants from Asia, follow their own traditions while also feeling a strong sense of identity as Canadian citizens.

▼ Celine Dion is the best-selling female recording artist in the world, with over 125 million albums sold. In 1999, Dion unveiled a plaque in her honor along Canada's Walk of Fame in Toronto.

A variety of well-stocked libraries, art galleries, and museums are found in all large Canadian cities. It is not just the large cities, however, that boast a rich culture. Few small towns in Canada are without a community theater or arts center with regular performances and exhibitions. The Canadian government promotes its unique heritage by recognizing the value of shared stories, poetry, knowledge, symbols, languages, customs, and traditions. These aspects of Canadian culture are seen as treasures that need to be kept alive and passed on to future generations.

Away from Canada's big cities, in remote rural areas, there tends to be less ethnic diversity, with more homogeneous small communities. Some First Nations people live on government-funded

▲ Some First Nations groups, particularly those along Canada's western coast, carve totem poles to tell stories about their communities. The figures show the importance of different community members. Each member has a carved symbol that is believed to be associated with a mystical nonhuman ancestor, often a wolf, a bear, an eagle, a whale, a salmon, or a raven.

▲ A fruit and vegetable market in Toronto's Chinatown. With residents from many different ethnic groups, cities like Toronto and Vancouver are extremely multicultural.

reservations in rural areas, where many follow their original traditions. Over 50 percent of First Nations people, however, now live in some of Canada's major cities, including Toronto, and many others live in the more remote cities such as Winnipeg in Manitoba. Urban First Nations people often face discrimination and social and economic challenges not usually experienced by other city-dwellers. However, with growing awareness and support from the Canadian government, an increasing number of young First Nations Canadians are attracted to the economic benefits and rich cultural diversity of city life.

HOLIDAYS AND FESTIVALS

Apart from the annual school and work holidays, Canadians enjoy ten national public holidays, as well as many individual provincial celebration days. In total, 250 festivals take place in Canada each year. Some of the national public holidays celebrate particular events, such as Labour Day, which commemorates the early recognition of trade unions in Canada in 1872. Other provincial festivals, such as the Maple Syrup festival in early April, celebrate old customs. The Maple Syrup festival marks the beginning of spring, and the people of Quebec and Ontario follow the tradition, started by the First Nations people, of boiling the sap of the maple tree to make syrup. Chinese New Year festivals are also a familiar feature in January in most Canadian cities.

DIFFERENT RELIGIOUS GROUPS

According to the 2001 census, around 45 percent of Canadians were Roman Catholic (with the majority of this group living in Quebec), and around 28 percent were Protestant. Within the Protestant population, some extreme groups enjoy the freedom to practice their religion in virtual isolation in this large and sparsely populated country.

For example, the Mennonites, a group originally founded in the early sixteenth

◀ The Canadian Tulip Festival is held in mid-May in Ottawa. Since World War II ended in 1945, the people of the Netherlands have sent one hundred thousand tulip bulbs to Ottawa each year to show their appreciation of Canada's help during the conflict. Canadian troops helped liberate the Netherlands, and the Dutch royal family found shelter in Canada during the war. Princess Margriet of the Netherlands, who was born in Ottawa, is shown here at the Fiftieth Canadian Tulip Festival in 2002.

century in the Netherlands by Menno Simmons, fled from persecution in Europe. One group of Mennonites, known as the Untere, were able to settle in Manitoba and live in peace. This group of Mennonites are relatively liberal. Few of them still wear their traditional clothes or work on communal farms.

The Ammanites, a more traditional Mennonite group, settled in Ontario, mainly in the Kitchener-Waterloo area to the east of Toronto. Unlike the Untere, they have shunned much of modern Canadian life. They do not use cars,

telephones, or modern machinery. They can often be seen in local towns, using horse-drawn carts and wearing their characteristic dark clothing, when they come to buy supplies.

Over the last few decades, waves of immigrants from Middle Eastern, Asian, and East African countries have brought their diverse religions with them. A total of sixty-three different religions, faiths, and sects are represented in Canada, and in 2001, there were thirty-four religions with more than 20,000 members each. In the cities, Muslim, Buddhist, Jewish, Hindu, and Sikh communities add to Canada's religious and cultural diversity. There are also a growing number of Canadians who declare themselves as atheist, agnostic, humanist, or non-religious. There are now 580,000 Canadian Muslims, who making up 2 percent of the country's population and represent the fastest-growing religion in Canada. (In 1991, Muslims made up only 0.9 percent of the Canadian population.) In contrast, Canadian membership in Christian churches is declining. In 2001, only 73 percent of Canadians belonged to either the Roman Catholic or the Protestant church. Ten years earlier, 83 percent of Canadians belonged to one of these churches.

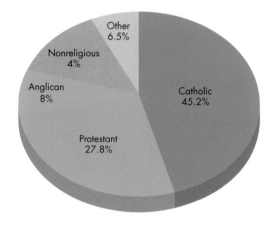

▲ Canada's major religions

Focus on: The Hutterites of Alberta

The Hutterites are an extreme Protestant group who have shunned the modern world almost totally. They refuse to vote and do not draw pensions or benefits from the Canadian government. About six thousand Hutterites live in close communities on the prairie plains of Alberta. They originated in Moravia, and their language is Hutterite, a form of German. They live in small communities of about one hundred

people. (When a Hutterite community reaches 150, another community is set up.) All their land is worked communally, and they all live in very simple, identical houses. Women and children eat together, and the men eat in a separate communal group. The women wear ankle-length, plain, dark-colored dresses and polka-dot scarves. The men wear dark suits and broad-brimmed hats. If they are married, Hutterite men wear beards.

CHAPTER 12

Leisure and Tourism

In Canada, outdoor activities, such as camping, walking, white-water rafting, canoeing, and skiing, are popular. Many Canadian families have cabins in the countryside, where they spend summer vacations. They may also go to these cabins in winter for hunting and skiing trips. Even large cities are within a short drive of open spaces, scenic landscapes, and coastal or lakeside beaches. Most towns and villages have a nearby lake or river teeming with fish. And all public parks, beaches, and parking areas on main roads have barbecue and picnic facilities.

WINTER SPORTS

Skiing is a popular leisure activity in eastern Canada, where the winters are very snowy. There are more than four hundred ski slopes

Tourism in Canada

- 🗁 Tourist arrivals, millions: 20
- 🗁 Earnings from tourism in U.S.$: 9,700,000,000
- 🗁 Tourism as % foreign earnings: 3
- 🗁 Tourist departures, millions: 17.7
- 🗁 Expenditure on tourism in U.S.$: 9,929,000,000

Source: World Bank

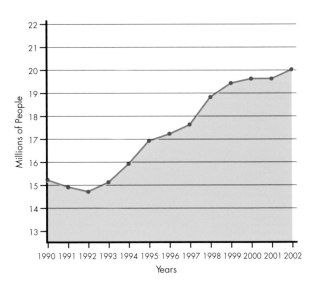

▲ Changes in international tourist arrivals, 1990–2002

◀ Whistler, near Vancouver, in British Columbia, is one of Canada's most popular ski resorts.

close to Montreal, and the city park, Mount Royal Park, is a particular favorite with families for casual skiing on winter weekends. On a grander scale, ski resorts in the Rockies, centered around Calgary and Whistler, offer some of the best facilities in the world and attract many European and American visitors.

Many Canadians also enjoy playing ice hockey, and Canada holds a leading position in world ice hockey competitions. The Canadian men's ice hockey team won the gold medal at the 2002 Winter Olympics in Salt Lake City.

Canadians are also well known in Olympic competition for excelling in rowing, swimming, cycling, trampolining, and many other sports. In the 2004 Olympics, held in Athens, Canadians won twelve medals, including three gold. The 1988 Winter Olympics were held in Calgary, and Vancouver will be the 2010 host.

SIGHT-SEEING AND ACTIVITY VACATIONS

Canada is vast, and journeys taken within the country cross a huge variety of landscapes and climates, from the frozen expanses of the Northwest Territories to the much warmer area of Vancouver on the Pacific coast. Canada has a great deal to offer tourists, including cities such as Toronto, with its CN Tower and Sky Dome; dramatic sights such as Niagara Falls; skiing in the Canadian Rockies; whale-watching on the banks of the St. Lawrence; and trekking through wilderness areas.

Canada also has many exciting theme parks. With so much land to spare, some of these

▼ Canada's Adam Van Koeverden wins the gold medal in men's K1 canoeing 500-meter race at the 2004 Olympic Games in Athens.

parks can boast that many of their attractions are the biggest of their kind. The Galaxy Park, near Edmonton, Alberta, is completely climate-controlled, with a huge 5-acre (2-hectare) water park kept at a balmy 85°F (29°C) all year round. In the same complex is the Ice Palace, which has a national hockey league sized ice rink. The Tomb Raiders' Flying Roller Coaster and other nerve-jarring movie-themed rides are located in Toronto's Paramount Wonderland theme park.

Tourists from Southeast Asia, where thriving economies have increased personal spending power, see Canada as a very appealing destination. The Japanese, in particular, are attracted to the resorts and cities of British Columbia, where city vacations in Vancouver and Calgary can be easily combined with visits to the nearby ski resorts of Calgary, Banff, and Lake Louise.

Tourist income is very important to Canada. In line with world trends, however, the number of overseas visitors dropped in 2002–2003. Global terrorism, the September 11 attacks on the United States, and the SARS outbreak all took their toll on international tourism, in general, and on travel to North American destinations, in particular. These events, however, have not had long-term effects on tourism and certainly not on travelers from the United States and on Canadians traveling within their homeland.

NATIONAL PARKS

Canada's national parks are a major destination for Canadians during their vacations. From the country's huge expanse of uninhabited land, the Canadian government has set aside thirty-eight national parks and national park reserves. (The reserves are areas over which there are unresolved land claims by indigenous peoples; these areas usually become officially designated national parks as soon as the claim is settled.)

The country's most popular parks are located in the Rocky Mountain provinces, where visitors can enjoy outdoor leisure activities including skiing, hiking, and camping. The spectacular scenery attracts both Canadians and visitors from all over the world. There are many other national parks all over Canada, and the National Parks and Wilderness Society protects many wilderness areas that are not designated as national parks. The parks are strictly

▲ Toronto has many attractions for visitors, including the CN Tower, shown here with Lake Ontario in the foreground. An elevator whisks visitors to the top of the tower at 1,197 feet (365 m) per minute—equal to the rate of ascent of a jet during take-off!

controlled to ensure a balance between visitor access and the preservation of natural habitats and landscapes. Any industries that extract materials from the Earth, such as mining or quarrying, are banned in Canada's national parks, and visitor access and the activities of visitors are carefully monitored. Canada's first national park, a 10 sq mile (26 sq km) area on the north slope of Mount Sulphur in the Rockies, was established in 1885. This area was later expanded, and it became the famous Banff National Park in 1887.

Focus on: Banff National Park

Banff, the best-known national park in Canada, is part of a UNESCO World Heritage site and covers 7,722 sq miles (20,000 sq km) of the Canadian Rocky Mountains. Its enormous popularity, its ecological and cultural importance, its contribution to the Canadian economy, and its service to visitors make it unique among Canada's national parks. The park management team has divided Banff's land into five different zones, with recreational activities tightly restricted in Zones 1, 2, and 3. Zone 4, which takes up only 1 percent of the land, is the main location for recreational activities. Zone 5, which also takes up only 1 percent of the park's land, contains the town of Banff and the Lake Louise complex, which holds most of the park's shops and visitor services. Notice boards around the park give instruction and advice to help ensure the safety of visitors and the preservation of wildlife habitats.

▼ Walkers stop to look at the bright blue Moraine Lakes near Lake Louise, in Banff National Park, Alberta, against the backdrop of the Rocky Mountains.

CHAPTER 13

Environment and Conservation

Canada's often inhospitable landscape and climate has helped preserve many of its remote wilderness areas. However, some of these wildernesses contain valuable resources, such as timber, that are in great demand. So Canada, like other resource-rich countries, is faced with the question of how to balance the need to protect its environment with the demand for jobs and economic development. With continuing pressure for economic development, environmental protection in such a huge country is a growing problem.

THE BRAZIL OF THE NORTH

Approximately 37 percent of Canada's land area is covered in forest, and deforestation is currently seen as the country's most serious environmental threat. It is estimated that two-thirds of the original old-growth forest in British Columbia has been cut down. Environmentalists criticize the clear-cutting method used in Canada's forests, which results in whole hillsides that are stripped of trees and left open to soil erosion. Canada has no significant green political party, but the Forest Processing Association is working with logging companies to encourage more sustainable practices. In addition, nongovernmental organizations, including the Rainforest Conservation Society, do research and publish articles on environmental issues affecting the rain forests of Vancouver Island and criticize the British Columbian government for not doing more to stop the destruction.

POLLUTION PROBLEMS

Only 11 percent of Canada's land is either populated or cultivated, but advances in technology and construction of access routes

▼ A forest on Vancouver Island, British Columbia, in which clear-cutting is being used.

have led to increasing expansion into remote areas. Although Canada has relatively few manufacturing industries for its size, many Canadians own cars and most of them make a large number of car journeys. So the country's rate of atmospheric pollution per person from greenhouse gases is high. On the positive side, Canada has pledged, along with most

developed countries, to reduce its CO_2 emissions. In addition, Montreal hosted a 1987 summit at which several countries agreed to phase out the use of chlorofluorocarbons (CFCs) in aerosols, refrigerators, and other products. CFCs harm Earth's protective ozone layer for up to one hundred years after they are released. By the time of the 1987 summit, Canada had already banned the use of CFCs in aerosols for nine years.

Even if the environmental damage caused by Canada's own economic development is reduced to a minimum, however, global pollution in the atmosphere and oceans would still affect Canada's delicately balanced ecosystems. Global pollution could affect the tundra and Arctic regions of Nunavut and the Northwest Territories, in particular. Because ice sheets are thinning as temperatures rise, these frozen lands and the habitats they support are becoming increasingly vulnerable to climate change.

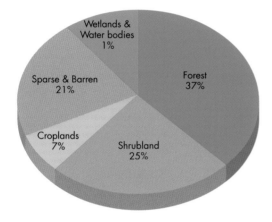

▲ Habitat type as percentage of total area

Environmental and Conservation Data

🗁 Forested area as % of total land area: 37

🗁 Protected area as % of total land area: 6.3

🗁 Number of protected areas: 5,285

SPECIES DIVERSITY

Category	Known species (1992–2002)	Threatened species (2002)
Mammals	193	14
Breeding birds	440	8
Reptiles	39	2
Amphibians	42	1
Fish	128	16
Plants	3,270	1

Source: World Resources Institute

◀ A herd of caribou runs across an open field in the Northwest Territories. Caribou are a very important source of meat and skins for the Inuit. Their breathable, waterproof hide is essential to hunters living in snowbound communities.

THREATS TO WILDLIFE

In the nineteenth century, the buffalo was almost hunted to extinction in Canada and the northern United States by Plains Indians and by white hunters. Historians have been very critical of how buffalo were hunted, but the same type of problem is occurring today with the reindeer that roam the frozen wilderness of northern Canada. Caribou numbers have fallen from about 2.5 million in the 1940s to about 700,000 today. The caribou is just one of the animals in danger of extinction today in Canada.

In 2004, newspapers around the world showed pictures of baby seals being clubbed to death off the coasts of Newfoundland and Labrador. This was reported to be the biggest cull of seals in fifty years. The media reports caused anger among wildlife conservation groups. But if the number of seals is not controlled, the seals will, in turn, decimate the fish stocks in Canada's east-coast waters. For this reason, the Canadian government allows hunters to kill 350,000 young seals each year. In 2004, critics felt that the culling

was excessive and was linked with the high prices paid by the fashion industry for seal pelts, which are made into a range of items, including coats, jackets, boots, and bags. The Canadian government argues that the seal-culling industry, which is worth twenty million Canadian dollars a year, is needed to support the economically troubled coastal towns on Canada's eastern seaboard, particularly those of Newfoundland. These towns have suffered economic losses from the decline in their fishing industry, which were mainly brought about by a 1992 ban on cod fishing. Over forty thousand people in the area lost their jobs, and property values dropped as people left the area to find new jobs. Recovery on Canada's eastern seaboard has been very slow.

Did You Know?

According to the WWF (formerly known as the World Wildlife Fund), summer sea ice in the Arctic is currently decreasing by 9.2 percent each decade. Because of this decrease, the polar bear and some seal species could be extinct by 2026.

Focus on: Polar Bears

Canada has about fifteen thousand polar bears, the largest polar bear population in any one country. These bears were once hunted almost to the point of extinction, but a treaty signed by the Arctic countries (Canada, the United States, Norway, Greenland, and Russia) in 1967 helped protect them. (The Inuit are allowed to hunt polar bears in limited numbers.) Unfortunately, polar bears are again under threat, this time because of global warming and industrial pollution. Many Canadian polar bears hunt in the Hudson-St. James Bay region, where—because of global warming—the frozen waters are now melting three weeks earlier than they did in 1980.

The earlier melt reduces the time polar bears have to hunt. In addition, pollutants in the water are eaten by fish, which are then eaten by polar bears. The pollutants concentrate in the bears' bodies and damage their immune systems. In recent years, scientists have also found a significant decrease in the size and weight of polar bears, and fewer polar bear cubs are being born.

◄ Two zoologists take samples from tranquilized polar bears to check the levels of pesticides in the bears' bodies, at Hudson Bay, Manitoba.

▼ A picture, taken in 2001, showing melting ice below Mount Leith, on Ellesmere Island, Nunavut.

CHAPTER 14

Future Challenges

At the beginning of the twenty-first century, Canada is a very prosperous, stable country. It has a low crime rate, and it is ranked in the twenty countries of the world with the fewest reported murders. In spite of this, it faces a number of economic, political, social, and environmental challenges.

A STRONG ECONOMY?

Canada's export trade is very strong, and China has become one of Canada's main customers. Exports to China are said to have risen 75 percent in the past few years. Over-dependence on the export of raw materials, however, could cause economic problems for Canada in the long term, particularly if the price of raw materials were to collapse. Expanding its manufacturing base would be a good way for Canada to diversify its economy, but labor and production costs in Canada are relatively high. As a result, some manufacturers in Canada have been moving their production to Mexico, where costs are lower.

SOCIAL AND ENVIRONMENTAL PROBLEMS

In an effort to balance national budgets, taxes and prices in Canada have been rising, and many people on low incomes have been

▼ Nonviolent protesters march to the Peace Bridge, which links Fort Erie, Ontario, in Canada, and Buffalo, New York, in the United States, in 2001 to protest against the Free Trade Area of Americas (FTAA) and North Atlantic Free Trade Agreement (NAFTA). Many U.S. companies are leaving Canada—and taking jobs with them—because NAFTA reduces tax advantages for them in Canada.

experiencing increasing financial problems. Welfare payments have also been cut, causing many indigenous people living in marginal, extreme environments, such as the Northwest Territories, to abandon their traditional lifestyles (which were supported by welfare payments) and move to Canada's main cities in search of reliable work. With all of Canada's major cities located in a belt close to the U.S. border, this concentration of cities in a relatively small area may, in the future, start to put too much pressure on land and resources in and around the U.S. border.

There are also some problems between particular groups within Canada, such as the First Nations people and the Canadians who are mostly of European origin, often over access to resources. The present government is working hard to bridge these divisions.

Canada is well known for encouraging a multicultural society. But, with a growing number of economic immigrants, and a government that has been accused of being too lax in controlling the flow of people into the country, public unease at Canada's immigration policy has been rising. Canada has a strict immigration policy for anyone applying to come in through official channels. Critics say, however, that, with such a long border and coastline, Canada has too many gaps through which people can enter illegally. The Canadian government is trying to address this problem by working in partnership with the U.S. government.

POLITICAL DIVISION

The possibility of Quebec separating from the rest of Canada is an issue that is not likely to disappear. The people of Quebec have had two referenda on this question, and those in favor of independence have been narrowly defeated. However, if Quebec does secede, Canada will lose not only its largest province but also the producer of a great deal of Canada's energy (in the form of hydroelectric power) and much of its industrial output. Keeping Quebec within Canada is going to be a major challenge for the future.

▼ A Canadian immigration officer gathers illegal Asian migrants as they prepare to board buses in Gold River, British Columbia, in 1999.

Time Line

25,000 B.C. Migrants start settling the land now known as Canada, mainly by crossing the land bridge that existed between the areas that are present-day Russia and Alaska.

1497 John Cabot, an Italian explorer, is given permission by Henry VII of England to set sail to Canada.

1534 Jacques Cartier, a French explorer, pioneers the first European settlement in Canada.

1670 King Charles II of England grants a Royal Charter to the Hudson's Bay Company for trapping and mineral rights on the land draining into Hudson Bay, known as Rupert's Land.

1759 The French are defeated by the British on the Plains of Abraham, just outside Quebec City. The French are then forced to give up the land around the St. Lawrence area and the Quebec settlements.

1763 France gives up all the land it holds in North America, including Quebec.

1846 The Oregon Treaty sets the forty-ninth parallel as the boundary between Canada and the United States.

1867 The North American Act creates the first confederation of Canada, which initially includes Nova Scotia, New Brunswick, and the British colonies then known as Canada.

1905 Alberta and Saskatchewan join the confederation.

1917 As allies of the British in World War I, Canadian soldiers are victorious at Vimy Ridge.

1949 Canada becomes a founding member of NATO.

1976 The Parti Quebecois wins the provincial election in Quebec, and French is made the official language in the province of Quebec.

Canada joins the G8 group of industrialized nations.

Montreal hosts the Olympic Games.

1982 Canada becomes fully independent when the British government transfers to Canada all powers relating to Canada in British law.

1988 Calgary hosts the Winter Olympics.

1992 Canada withdraws its troops from European bases.

1994 NAFTA takes effect.

1995 The people of Quebec narrowly reject separation from the rest of Canada.

1999 Nunavut is created as a separate territory.

2003 Paul Martin becomes Canada's prime minister.

Nova Scotia and Prince Edward Island are hit by Hurricane Juan, the worst hurricane to hit an inland location so far north.

SARS outbreak in Toronto.

2004 At the Olympic Games in Greece, Canada wins twelve medals, including three gold medals.